Me & God

A Book of Partner Prayers

Deb Lund

illustrated by Carolyn Digby Conahan

MOREHOUSE PUBLISHING
A Continuum imprint
HARRISBURG · LONDON · NEW YORK

Morehouse Publishing
A Continuum Imprint

4775 Linglestown Road
Harrisburg, Pennsylvania 17112
www.morehousepublishing.com

Cover design by Trude Brummer
Page design by Trude Brummer

A catalog record of this book is available
from the Library of Congress.

ISBN 0-8192-1911-8

Printed in Malaysia

03 04 05 06 07 08   6 5 4 3 2 1

For the Erlanders,
and all who "share prayers"
with those they love.

Thank you, God!

For bugs and birds and rocks and trees,
Thank you, God!

For kisses on my scraped-up knees,
Thank you, God!

For food and friends and family,
Thank you, God!

For all the love you give to me,
Thank you, God!

I will bless you, God, and I will not forget the wonderful things you do for me. —Psalm 103:2

God Be In Me

    God, be in me
to help me know
where you would like my feet to go.

    God, be in me
throughout the day
in all I do and all I say.

    God, be in me
so others see
how loved and cared for they can be.

Teach me your way, God,
and I will walk in your truth.
—Psalm 86:11

God Comes Along With Me

Riding with my family,
To the city, woods, or sea,
    God comes along with me.

In a boat, a bus, or train,
When I'm flying in a plane,
    God comes along with me.

On a bike, a hike, a slide,
Even on a wagon ride,
    God comes along with me.

*You search out my path and my
resting and know all my ways.
—Psalm 139:3*

Everywhere

God is here. God is there.
Where is God?
Everywhere.

In those who give us loving care,
Could God be there?
Everywhere.

In hope, in joy, in hurt, in fear.
Would God be there?
Everywhere.

Thank you, God, for being near.
Is God right here?
Everywhere.

*I am with you and will
keep you wherever you go.
—Genesis 28:15*

God Loves Me

It's as simple as can be,
    God loves me.

Easier than one, two, three,
    God loves me.

When I'm good or when I'm bad,
    God loves me.

When I'm happy, mad, or sad,
    God loves me.

Each and every night and day,
    God loves me.

No matter what I do or say,
    God loves me.

Nothing can separate us
from the love of God.
—Romans 8:38

Amen

God of water, land, and air,
Your name is special. Hear my prayer.
Amen.

Help me choose how I should be,
Forgiving all as you do me.
Amen.

Feed us, keep us in your care,
And help us learn to really share.
Amen.

You will lead us, strong and true,
Today and always, only you!
Amen.

God knows what you
need before you ask.
—Matthew 6:8

God Smiles at Me

When friends and I are out at play,
  God smiles at me.

When I don't have a perfect day,
  God smiles at me.

And in the faces that I see,
  God smiles at me.

And in the mirror, could it be?
  God smiles at me.

We are many parts.
We are all one body.
—1 Corinthians 12:12

Love, Love, Love

God stays here beside me to comfort and guide me,
But what I love most is God's
    Love, Love, Love.

God knows who I am, and God knows how I've been,
And God still keeps on giving me
    Love, Love, Love.

At times when I'm angry, afraid or so sad,
I just try to remember God's
    Love, Love, Love.

I can't do a thing to erase it or change it,
God never stops giving me
    Love, Love, Love.

*How precious is
your constant love.
—Psalm 36:7*

God Believes in Me

God believes in me.
When I'm feeling ten feet tall,
And even when I'm scared and small.

God believes in me.
When I'm sure where I belong,
And even when I'm not so strong.

God believes in me.
When I forget that God is there,
And even as I say this prayer.
God believes in me.

*I have loved you with
a never-ending love and
have been faithful to you.*
—Jeremiah 31:3

Good Night, God

I'm tired, God, you understand.
Will you please stay and hold my hand?
  Good night, God.

Snuggle in and hug me tight.
Keep me safe all through the night.
  Good night, God.

God bless Mama, Daddy, too.
Remind us that we're loved by you.
  Good night, God.

I'll lie here without a peep,
Because you're with me while I sleep.
  Good night, God.

*I will lie down in
peace and sleep, for
God will keep me safe.
—Psalm 4:8*

Deb Lund is a children's author and a certified classroom, music, and library teacher, and the founding director of Cedar Educational Partnerships, an arts-integrated home school support program. She's also led storytelling troupes, directed choirs, and performed with a trio of musicians called "The Basics." Her talents and enthusiasm have led her to teach courses to kids and adults in her community and elsewhere—everything from nature study to canoeing to music to writing. In her free time, she enjoys singing, hiking, kayaking, dancing, and drawing. Deb lives on an island in Puget Sound with her musician husband and their six-year-old son.

Carolyn Digby Conahan studied at Reed College and at the Pacific Northwest College of Art. Her illustrations have appeared in a variety of children's publications, from *Highlights for Children* to *LadyBug, Spider,* and *Cricket* magazines. She's also done wildlife illustrations for *Oregon Wildlife* and other publications. She lives with her husband and children in Portland, Oregon.